AMAZING MAGIC™

MAGIC of the MIND

Tricks for the Master Magician

Paul Zenon

rosen publishing's
rosen
central®

New York

North American edition first published in 2008 by:

The Rosen Publishing Group, Inc.
29 East 21st Street
New York, NY 10010

North American edition book design: Nelson Sá
North American edition editor: Nicholas Croce
Photography: Karl Adamson (tricks), Rich Hardcastle (remaining images)

Library of Congress Cataloging-in-Publication Data

Zenon, Paul.
Magic of the mind: tricks for the master magician / Paul Zenon.—North American ed.
    p. cm.—(Amazing magic)
Contains material previously published in *Street Magic*, © 2005.
Includes bibliographical references and index.
ISBN-13: 978-1-4042-1072-1 ISBN-1-4042-1759-2 (pbk)
ISBN-10: 1-4042-1072-5
1. Magic tricks—Juvenile literature. I. Zenon, Paul. *Street Magic*. II. Title. III. Series.

GV1548.Z46 2008
793.8—dc22

                                                                2007010353

Manufactured in Singapore

CONTENTS

INTRODUCTION

The ultimate arena for magic is the mind. When you perform a magic trick, the audience is baffled, but they know that their amazement is the result of your skills. However, when you present a mind-reading trick, audiences seem to take it at face value—they genuinely want to believe that such a thing is possible. Be prepared for that. Remember that magic doesn't happen in your hands; it happens in the mind of the audience. And, after you've performed a few tricks from this book, don't be surprised if people start standing in line to have their palms read!

There's no better audience than party-goers, but the tricks have to play big so that the whole room can appreciate them. These mind magic tricks are some of my favorites—killer routines designed to make your audience whoop with laughter or scream in surprise. Don't do them all at once, though—always hold one trick back because if the party starts to die down, you're sure to be asked to do one more piece of magic. That's when you hit them with your very best trick—the one that'll have you remembered long after the party's forgotten.

TRICK 1

This is an anywhere, anytime miracle of prophecy in which you predict which one of half a dozen objects on a table someone will choose. This trick is clever. Once you understand the principle, it can be used in various ways. Here, it's used to make a spectator choose a specific object from the six on the table. As well as half a dozen different items, you'll also need a pen and paper to make your prediction with.

Let's assume you're at a party. You tell everyone you want to try an experiment and you start to clear the table before putting six different objects on it: a glass, bottle, watch, coaster, spoon, fork. It doesn't actually matter what they are.

Write the name of one of the objects on a piece of paper without anyone seeing and fold it up and give it to someone to hold. "Don't read it yet," you say. We'll imagine that you've written, "You will choose the coaster" on the paper. "This isn't magic. It's psychology. It's the kind of thing the military uses to instill obedience in its soldiers. So, I want you to follow my instructions very closely and very quickly: what happens might just surprise you."

Pick out someone to help you and then ask him to look over the objects. Call out the items one at a time. "When I snap my fingers, I want you to pick up two of the objects immediately, one in each hand. I'll point to one of them and you just get rid of it; just hand it to one of the guys here as quickly as you can. Place the other one back on the table. Got it?" Assuming he's understood you, snap your fingers and he picks up two objects. It doesn't matter which two he picks; you point to one and tell him to throw it to one of the other spectators.

However, if he picks up the coaster, the object you've predicted, you always point to the other object and he always puts the coaster back on the table. This is the only important thing you need to remember. There are now five objects on the table. One's been eliminated. "OK, my turn." You quickly pick up any two objects—any except the coaster—and hold them up one in each hand for the spectator to see. "Point to the one you want me to throw away. The other goes back on the table."

He points to one, and you throw it to the other spectators and put the remaining object back on the table. "Quick: again. Pick up two objects." He does, and again you point to one and he throws it away and puts the remaining object back on the table.

Once again, if one of the objects he chose was the coaster, make sure you point to the other one. There are now three objects on the table. Pick up the two that aren't the coaster. He points to one and you throw it away, placing the other one back down. Ask him to take the last two objects, one in each hand. As he does, you turn your back on him, casually noting in which hand he takes the coaster as you do so. "OK, one last time. Throw away the object in your . . ." Pause here for effect and then say, "Right hand. What are you left with?" In fact, you already know where the coaster is, so you can safely tell him to throw the object that's in the other hand away. But if you get the timing right on this, people will think that you turned away before he picked up the objects and, therefore, couldn't have had any idea which hand held which object.

Tell him to put the last object behind his back. Turn around to face him. He's holding the coaster out of sight, a move that again psychologically helps give the impression that you're not sure which object he's left with. "Did you notice what I was doing? You hardly had time to think—you picked up two objects, chose one, and threw the other away. Which object are you left with?" He reveals the coaster. Try to look as if you're a bit surprised. Then ask the spectator who's holding your prediction to read it out. It says, "You will choose the coaster."

NOTES

As previously mentioned, the force used in this routine, devised by British magician Roy Baker, can be used in many different ways. Here are just a couple.

First, you don't have to write your prediction down. You could secretly attach a sticker with the words "You will choose this" written on it to the bottom of any one of the objects. That's the object you avoid during the forcing procedure. Get the spectator to turn the final object over to reveal your secret message. All the people holding the discarded objects will now turn them over, too, thinking they must all have a similar sticker. They'll be amazed that the chosen object is the only one.

Take half a dozen envelopes and secretly mark one of them by nicking it at the corner with your nail. You mark it just enough so that you can tell it apart from the others. To perform the routine, borrow a dollar bill and seal it in the marked envelope. You put pieces of paper into the other envelopes.

Go through the force procedure and this time have the spectators put them through a shredding machine. Naturally you avoid discarding the marked envelope at every turn. Whoever loaned you the money will be relieved to find that the last envelope chosen contains his or her cash.

Apply your imagination and see what other interesting variations you can come up with.

TRICK 2

Graphology is the analysis of a person's handwriting to reveal his or her character. In this trick, you accurately analyze the writing of four total strangers.

You can present this trick in an informal setting with a few people gathered around a table, but it's also big enough to include in a larger show. In this example, we'll assume that you have an average-sized audience in front of you.

You'll also need four pieces of paper and four envelopes. The pieces of paper are ordinary, but three of the envelopes have been marked by placing fingernail marks at their edges (1). The fingernail marks have been highlighted in black in the photo. The first envelope is marked at the top edge, the second on the right side, and the third on the left side. You can identify the fourth envelope by the fact that it's the only one that isn't marked.

Notice, too, that the fingernail marks are all marked on the flap side of the envelopes, so you know which side to look for them on.

Hand the envelopes out to four people, making sure you know who has which one. It's easiest to think of handing the envelopes out to your spectators from left to right, with envelope number one being given to the left-most volunteer and so on round to the right.

Hand them each a sheet of paper and a pen and tell them that in a minute you're going to play a game of word association. You'll mention three words, and then you want them to think of any single word that comes to mind and write it down on their piece of paper. Then they're to fold the paper in half and put it inside the envelope. They should try not to let anyone see the word they've written. When they understand this, you start the word association game.

"Listen carefully. Here are the words. 'Apple.' That's the first word. Here's the next word: 'sun.' And here's the last word: 'blue.' Apple, sun, blue. Now I'm going to turn around and I want you to write down any word that comes to mind. OK, do it now." You turn your back to the volunteers and they write down their words.

Wait a few moments, and then tell them to fold their papers and put them into the envelopes and seal them. Then they pass them to a completely independent person who mixes the envelopes up.

"Tell me when you've done that." You turn around and take the envelopes and now you begin to spin a yarn. "We're playing a game of word association. You know, it's amazing how much you can tell about a person by what word they think of." Take one of the envelopes and open it, take out the paper, and read the word. "Not to mention the way they write it . . ." Don't show the paper to anyone else at this stage.

As you open the envelope, you note the position of your marking. This tells you which person wrote the word inside. You're about to give a character reading about that person based, supposedly, on her handwriting and her choice of word. In actual fact, you have a distinct and unfair advantage because you know who that person in your audience is. Take a hard look at her and try to work out what kind of a person she is. Let's assume this one is young, fashionable, smart, and with her boyfriend.

Here's the kind of thing you could say. "Interesting choice of word. And even more interesting is the way it was written. Some people use their best handwriting, some people use capital letters, some I can hardly read at all, but this word is written very, very clearly, almost like they're filling in an official form. The lines and curves tell me a lot, too. This is a person who likes to be in control but also has a soft side; likes to be the boss but also likes affection.

"It shows a neat and orderly character—youthful, too. Probably considers themselves to be quite trendy, and, I think, quite possibly in love at the moment. Let me try to go a bit further. It's definitely written by a female. I reckon she'd be fashionable and quite pretty— and already in a relationship. Just remind me again which of you wrote words down: can you all put your hands up, please?" The four people raise their hands.

As soon as they do, everyone will be looking to see which one is the young, pretty, fashionable girl you've been talking about. Pick her out of the four people, saying, "I think it could very well be you. What word did you write?" She calls out her word and you immediately turn the paper around to show that you're correct. "One down, three to go. Let's try a second word."

Open another envelope and again note the marking. Again, this tells you which of your volunteers wrote the word. "Let's try this differently. I want everyone who wrote something to keep a straight poker face. I'm going to show you the word." Turn the paper around and reveal the word to the audience. You can get some fun out of this no matter what word has been written. Remind everyone that you called out three words at the beginning: apple, sun, and blue. Now read out the word that's written on the paper.

It might be something that follows your words in a logical fashion or it might be something totally out of left field. Whichever it is, make the most of it. For example: "So, I called out 'apple,' 'sun,' and 'blue,' and that made one of you guys think of 'wine.' Now, why would anyone think of 'wine'? Perhaps there's some obvious connection between wine and those three words that I'm not making? Is it because you're holding a glass of wine? Or maybe it's your answer to everything? Are we looking at a connoisseur or someone who needs professional help?"

You're just having a bit of fun with the reading, but now you pretend to get a little more serious, as during the above you've sized up the spectator who wrote the word. Let's assume it's a middle-aged man. Your reading might go something like this: "So, 'wine': a sophisticated drink, and so possibly written by a sophisticated person— someone who appreciates the finer things in life. Probably someone with a little worldly wisdom: not someone who's immature, someone more experienced in life. And written in a very masculine hand; definitely written by a man . . . and I think that man was you." At this point, look directly at the guy who wrote the word.

He admits that it was indeed him. That leaves two words left. You open both envelopes and take out both sheets of paper, mentally noting which sheet belongs to which of the two remaining volunteers. Ask the two people to raise their hands for a moment and then ask them their occupations. "OK—retail manager and financial analyst. That'll give me something to work on."

You could end the trick right here and reveal who wrote which, but it wouldn't be all that effective. It would be more likely to look like the trick that it is, rather than genuine psychology. You have to convince everyone that you're now using the information the volunteers have just given you to assess the two different words on the papers. Read the words out to the audience, "'Door' and 'lemon.' Two very different words and two very different people. The first word is written in a hand that's very bold, very solid: capital letters again. The second is written in a flowing script—large loops, denoting honesty—while the straight lines of the capitals show strength of personality. Let me try one more thing." Look at the volunteers and say, "I want you both to name a color. You first. When I snap my fingers, call out a color. And now you. Any color, just call it out."

It doesn't matter what colors they call out; this is just pure showmanship to help give the impression that you're somehow using psychological means again to determine who wrote which word. Pause dramatically, then bring the trick to a close by handing each sheet to the correct person, "'Door' is yours, I believe. And that means that you're the lemon!" You're right on both counts.

NOTES

This trick depends on being convincing. You have to be able to make numerous general statements about people's character after taking just a brief look at them and then tie these statements into your routine. A good way to practice is just to sit somewhere and look at the people around you. What would you say about them if they were helping out with the routine?

Magicians call this kind of character analysis "cold reading," and there are lots of books written about it. It's the main tool used by many so-called psychics. Essentially, it's about making very general and mostly flattering statements to people who subjectively believe that they apply very specifically to them.

If you look at this trick, you'll see that you actually tell the spectators very little, yet they'll be drawn in because they really do believe that you're analyzing what their word and handwriting might reveal about them. And because you only ever say reasonably flattering things about them—being strong or fashionable or attractive, for example—they'll find it hard to disagree with anything you say! It's part of the magic that makes psychological and "psychic" routines believable. If you have a gift for improvisation and are good at flattery, chances are you'll make a good mind reader!

TRICK 3

Y ou show a royal flush in spades and invite someone to choose one of the five cards. He remembers it and the hand of cards is shuffled back into the deck. Then you reveal that it was no ordinary hand of cards: it was the hand that Wild Bill Hickok was apparently dealt just before he was shot dead at the card table. It's been known as the Dead Man's Hand ever since.

You offer to invoke the spirit of Wild Bill in order to find the selected card. You spell out the words "Wild Bill" and "Dead Man's Hand," dealing a card for each letter. The very next card in the deck turns out to be the card that the spectator chose: a very strange coincidence.

But that's not all. A spectator deals five hands of poker as you tell everyone that when the spirit of Wild Bill is invoked, the Dead Man's Hand has a habit of falling to the person whose back is toward the door. Everyone takes a look at the cards they've been dealt. Suddenly there's a loud bang!

When everyone's calmed down they see that the man nearest the door has indeed been dealt a royal flush—in spades. This is a really fun routine to perform. Begin by offering to tell a strange story. "It's the story of Wild Bill Hickok. Wild Bill was a gambler. In fact, he actually died at the card table, and the hand of cards he held at that time has been known ever since as the Dead Man's Hand. And this was it."

Spread the deck with the faces toward you as you look for the royal flush in spades: the ten, jack, queen, king, and ace. Separate these five cards from the rest of the deck by pulling them out slightly from the rest of the deck wherever you locate them: this is known as an "upjog." As you look for these cards, you are also counting down sixteen cards from the face of the deck, secretly putting a crimp in the lower left corner of the seventeenth card with your thumb (1).

Don't include any of the royal flush cards in your count if they fall within this block of seventeen. Don't panic; this isn't as difficult as it sounds, but if you're worried, you can do it secretly before you even start the trick. Close up the deck, pull out the royal flush, and drop them face-up onto the table. "The royal flush in spades; many people consider it the most prestigious hand in poker. But it was also the hand that killed Wild Bill. Give them a shuffle." Hand the royal flush to one of the spectators and ask him to mix the cards, face-down. When he's finished, you ask him to square up the packet and take a secret peek at the bottom card. "Remember that card; it'll be important later." Let's assume he saw the ace of spades. With your right hand, cut the deck at the crimp you made and drop the upper half onto the table. Tell the spectator to drop his cards on top of it. You then drop the remainder of the deck on top of the others. Square the deck and

ask the spectator to give it a complete cut. You then pick up the deck and give it a few more cuts, finishing by cutting your crimp to the bottom.

The position now is that the royal flush is below the sixteen cards you secretly counted to earlier. "Gamblers are generally superstitious people: Wild Bill was no exception. They tend to trust little rituals to bring them luck. Here's one." You start to deal out four hands of cards, from left to right across the table. You call out a letter for each card dealt, "W-I-L-D. That's the first word." Deal out a second round of cards on top of the first, again calling out a letter for each card dealt. "B-I-L-L. That's the second." Deal three more rounds of cards until you've got four hands of five cards on the table. As you deal each card you spell a letter, "D-E-A-D M-A-N-S H-A-N-D." Look at the spectator who chose the card and ask him to name it. Turn over the top card of the deck. It'll be his selection, the ace of spades (2).

"It looks like Wild Bill is with us. Let's see if we can take it a little bit further." Turn the chosen card face-down on top of the deck. Then gather up the four dealt hands of cards and drop them on top of the deck. It doesn't matter in which order you gather the hands so long as you don't disturb the order of the cards in any individual hand. Amazingly, the deck is now set up for you to deal out five poker hands with the first hand dealt consisting of a royal flush in spades. "Let's play five hands of poker," you say. "Why don't you deal?" Before handing the deck over, you've mentally selected one of the spectators. It will be the spectator who's sitting with his back directly to the nearest door. Since the first hand dealt will contain the royal flush, you hand the deck to the person to his immediate right. Then choose five people who should be dealt cards. Naturally, this includes the man who's going to deal. He deals

the first card to the man to his left and continues dealing left to right, dealing the fifth card to himself.

Let him carry on dealing five poker hands this way. "In a moment I want you to look at your hands, but first let me tell you this: the legend of the Dead Man's Hand says that the royal flush in spades will always fall to the man with his back to the door. Let's see if it's true."

As soon as the spectators pick up their hands of cards, you clap your hands really loudly to mimic the sound of the gunshot that killed Wild Bill. If you've built up the atmosphere sufficiently, the clap should make them jump out of their seats. As they recover, they'll see that the guy with his back to the door has indeed been dealt the Dead Man's Hand.

NOTES

This brilliant plot was originated many years ago by the magician Henry Christ. He used a hand of cards consisting of eights and aces, which, according to legend, was the actual hand held by Wild Bill at the time of his death. Personally I think that a royal flush in spades is more obvious and memorable, especially as most people know that the ace of spades is popularly known as the Death Card.

TRICK 4

This little miracle makes it look as if you have the ability to move objects with the power of your mind. Just by concentrating, you make an ordinary key slowly revolve on your outstretched hand. And the best thing about it is that it's really easy to do.

You'll need an ordinary mortice key that's slightly longer than the width of your palm. The part that goes into the lock is known as the "bit." At the other end of the key is the "handle," a simple oval with a hole through the middle—this needs to be wide and heavy in relation to the bit. Lay the key across your open palm so that the bit is on your hand pointing toward you. The handle extends over the edge of the palm (1).

"This key was given to me by my grandfather. He told me it was the key to a haunted house. I believed him, but then I was only

six at the time. I don't really think it's the key to a haunted house. I don't even believe in haunted houses. But that doesn't mean there isn't something a little strange about it. Look."

Hold your hand out so that everyone can see the key clearly. "Focus your mind on that key. Just for a second, imagine that it really does belong to a haunted house. Watch." Now slowly tip your hand ever so slightly so that the fingers dip imperceptibly toward the floor. If you have the right key, it will be so finely balanced that even the slightest tipping movement will cause it to revolve on your palm (2).

Take it slow and easy: you don't want anyone to spot that you're tipping your hand. And keep up your storyline to build the spooky atmosphere.

"That's it, look. Slowly the key moves by itself, as if turned by an invisible hand." Once the key has started to revolve, it'll continue until it has rotated 180 degrees and it'll tend to speed up once it's past the halfway point. You can slow it down by tipping your hand back slightly the other way. "That's it—done."

"And you know what the really weird thing is? When you get home, you'll find your back door unlocked. And if my grandfather's

ghost has been around, your television will probably have been gone, too!"

NOTES

You apparently can prove to the audience that you're not moving your hand. Simply ask someone to hold your fingertips (3). It makes no difference. Just raise your wrist instead of dipping your fingers to make the key turn. And take your time—the slower the key turns, the spookier it looks.

TRICK 5

I n this scary routine, the dead seem to make themselves known, and you appear to temporarily become one of them! Half a dozen folded slips of paper have the names of people who are alive written on them, but one paper has the name of a person who's dead. They're mixed up, and yet you're able to divine the name of the dead person by a very strange method—when you touch that particular piece of paper, your pulse stops!

There are two different elements to this trick. The first is the method for making the pulse in your wrist stop. All you need to do is hide a golf ball or similar-sized object under your left armpit. Take the pulse in your left wrist; if you're normal and healthy, it will beat away with a regular rhythm. When you want to stop your pulse, just gently squeeze your arm against the golf ball. The flow of blood to the wrist will stop and you might be surprised to find that your pulse just fades away to an apparent standstill (1).

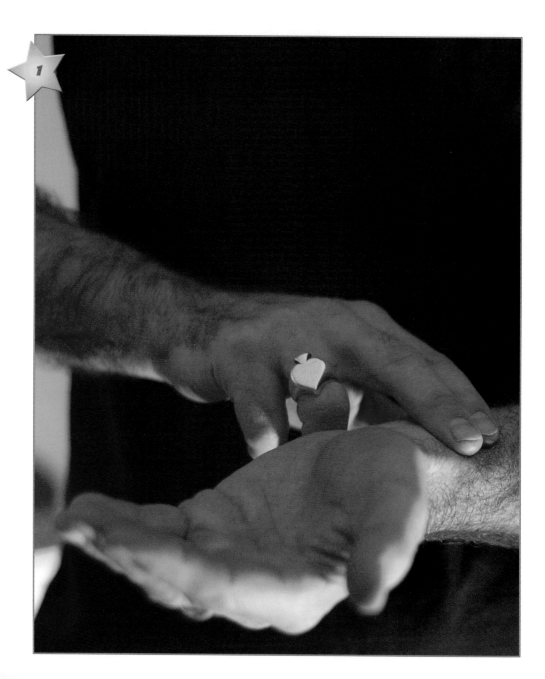

You'd normally wear a jacket or have the ball inside your shirt. Obviously, you don't want to be walking around all day clenching a golf ball under your armpit on the off-chance that someone might ask you to show him a trick. So, put it in a small bag and then safety-pin it to the inside of your jacket sleeve, or tape it to your shirt. That way, it's ready whenever you decide to perform the routine.

The second element of the trick is how you know which slip of paper has the dead name written on it. The answer lies in the pieces of paper: one of them is marked so that you can pick it out from the rest. There are lots of ways of marking the paper, but this is a particularly clever one. It uses a small, wire-bound notepad.

Take a craft knife and make clean slits at the top of the first page, between the punched holes that the binding goes through and the top edge of the paper. When you tear this page out, it will look very different from the others because of the straight cuts. The holes in other pages torn from the book will be more uneven and ragged; you'll see the difference in the photo. Here the holes with slits are to the left and right, with torn ones in the middle for comparison (2).

If you don't want to use paper, try using postcards or the blank sides of business cards. Mark one of the cards on its edge by running the tip of a pencil along it. The markings only can be read if you tip the card edge-on toward you. Mark it on both long edges so that you can always read it without having to turn the card around.

Now that you understand the basic principles, let me describe the routine in more detail because, as always, it's the way you present the trick that's going to make it effective. Take out the pad and some pens and say, "They say dead men tell no tales, but that's not true—let me

show you." Tear out some pages from the notepad—six is plenty—and hand one to each of six spectators.

Be sure that you know who receives the marked paper. "I'd like you to think of someone close to you, but someone I couldn't know. And then I'll turn my back and I want you to write the name of that person on the piece of paper. Let me know when you've finished."

The spectators are ready to begin their task but you stop them, saying, "Oh, and one more thing—I want everyone to write the name of someone who's still alive today . . . everyone except you!" Point to the person who has the marked paper, saying, "I want you to write down the name of someone who's dead." There's a macabre tone to the request.

Turn your back while the spectators write down names. When they've finished, tell them to fold the papers in half and then ask someone to gather them and mix them up so that no one knows which one is which. You can now turn around again. This is when you ask for a volunteer to take your pulse; if you're wearing the ball under your left arm, then have the person stand on your left side. Extend your left arm, bending it at the elbow, and ask the person to take your pulse. If he is doing it properly you'll have your left hand palm-up and he will have his fingers on your wrist—he should use his fingers, not his thumb. After a few moments he should be able to detect your steady pulse. "How am I?" you ask, jokingly. With any luck, he will say that you seem just fine.

Ask someone to give you one of the slips of paper. Take it in your right hand and hold it to your forehead, but as you do so, get a glimpse of the torn edge of the paper. You're looking for those telltale straight cuts—if you don't see them, concentrate for a little while purely for effect and then ask the spectator for a report on your pulse.

Of course, it's still normal. Hold the paper out, crush it into a ball, and drop it to the floor. "Let me know if you feel anything different," you say to the spectator who's holding your wrist.

One at a time you take the slips of paper and hold them to your forehead before asking for a report on your well-being. When you see that you've got the marked slip in your hand, squeeze your arm slowly against the hidden ball. Your pulse will gradually fade away before coming to a stop. This won't escape the notice of the spectator holding your wrist. You don't need to say anything; the expression on his face will say it all. Pause, then take a deep breath and silently hand the slip to someone nearby.

At the same time, relax your left arm. Your pulse returns the moment the slip is put down. Let your assisting spectator confirm this, then pick up the slip again. Your pulse disappears once more. The spectator will find this deeply disturbing. Look at the slip of paper and ask, "Who wrote the dead person's name?" Let that person identify himself. Using both hands, open the paper toward you and read the name to yourself, then ask the person to tell everyone the name. As he does, you dramatically turn the paper so that everyone can see you are holding the dead person's name in your hands. Hand the slip back to the person, saying, "If I were you, I wouldn't hold on to it for too long!"

NOTES

You can use the business of stopping your pulse in a variety of ways. For instance, you could use it in combination with Trick 4; as the key rotates on one hand a spectator feels the pulse in your other wrist slowly come to a deathly stop.

The tricks in this book have been chosen to give you material that can be changed, altered, and varied to suit your personal style and taste. Part of the joy of magic is creating routines that are your own. It's your chance to perform things no one has seen before. Make the most of that opportunity.

TRICK 6

In this baffling trick, you appear to foretell the future. You predict in advance a date, a name, and a playing card, which each of three spectators will select. And you're 100 percent accurate each time.

This routine uses what's known as the "one-ahead principle," although, as you'll see, it should really be named the "one-behind principle." It's been the building block of many a good mind-reading routine and you'll soon be using it to create your own.

For now, though, just follow the routine as described so that you can understand the workings. The theme is fortune-telling and you have some coins, a deck of playing cards, a pad of paper, and a pen. You also need a cup or mug or even a baseball cap—any kind of receptacle into which you can place the three predictions.

Shuffle the deck of cards and then place it face-down nearby, but, as you do so, catch a glimpse of the bottom card. Let's assume it's the three of clubs. Make sure that no one else sees this card.

Start the routine as a conversation about fortune-telling. Ask the spectators if they've ever had their fortunes told. "Someone might have drawn up an astrological chart, read your palm, or maybe you broke open a fortune cookie, and whatever it said inside freaked you out a bit. I don't believe that it's actually possible to tell the future, but let me show you an interesting little experiment."

You're going to use three people for this trick. Let's assume that Bob is the first. Look him over as if trying to figure something out about his future and then write "Three of clubs" on the top sheet of the pad. Don't let anyone see the writing. Tear the sheet off and fold it into quarters with the writing inside. On the outside of the folded paper write the number 3 (1). Don't tell anyone what you're doing, just do it and then drop the paper into the cup or hat, making sure that no one can see the number you wrote.

Now ask Bob to think of a month of the year. It can be the month of his birthday, his wedding anniversary, graduation, or anything else. All you ask is that the month has some significance to him. "Which month did you choose?" He tells you and you ask him why he chose that particular month. Let's assume he chose May because that's when his birthday is. Frankly it doesn't matter to you at all, but it gives you a reason for him to tell you the month he's thinking of without arousing his suspicions. Move on to the second spectator, Suzie. Ask her to think of a name; nothing too obscure. It should be the name of someone she knows, but not the name of anyone present. "And no pets," you say, as if anticipating her trying to make things difficult for you.

Look into her eyes as if trying to see that name. Then write something on the pad. Everyone there thinks that you're writing a name. In fact you're writing the month of "May" that Bob thought of. Make sure no one sees your writing, or you'll be busted before

you start. Tear off the sheet, fold it into quarters as before, and write the number 1 on the side of the folded slip.

Drop the paper into the cup along with the first folded paper. You now can ask Suzie to reveal the name of the person she was thinking of. Let's assume she tells you that she was thinking of Jake, the name of her ex-boyfriend. Make the relationship seem important. It'll disguise the fact that you're merely interested in finding out the name. As an aside, ask if she knows someone called John. You'll see why later.

Turn to the third spectator. "Steve, I want to try something different with you; not a month or a name or anything else that might already be in your mind. Let's pick something by chance instead." Pick up the pad, look at Steve, and then write "John or Jake" on the top sheet. Tear the sheet off, fold it into quarters, and then, again out of view of the spectators, write a number 2 on the side before dropping it into the cup. Now ask Steve to cut the deck of playing cards into two heaps. Take what was the lower portion of the deck and put it cross-ways on top of the other portion (2). As you do this, you say, "Let's just mark the cut." Later you'll see how this maneuver, known as the cross-cut force, is used to force the original bottom card of the deck, the three of clubs, onto Steve.

"OK," you say, "three predictions, three people. Let's see how we've done." Tip the three folded slips from the cup onto the table. Put slip number 1 in front of Bob, slip number 2 in front of Suzie, and slip number 3 in front of Steve. This is the first time the spectators see the numbers you wrote on the sides of the slips. "Bob, I asked you to choose a month. You chose the month of your birthday. When is that again?" He tells you that it's May. You open the slip of paper in front of him to reveal that May was the month you predicted.

"Suzie, I asked you to think of someone close. You thought of your ex. What was his name?" She reminds everyone that it was Jake. You open the slip of paper and she sees that you wrote down the names Jake and John. The extra name makes it look like you weren't quite sure. It's a convincing touch, since the name Jake is clearly there all the same. And it's not that dissimilar to John. It has to be more than coincidence.

"Steve, I didn't ask you to think of anything; I said that we'd let chance take a hand. Let's look at the card you cut to." You reach over and lift up the top half of the deck and turn it over to reveal the face card (3). It's the three of clubs. In actual fact, the three of clubs was the original bottom card of the deck, but so much has happened since the cut was made that no one remembers which packet was where.

Ask Steve to open the slip of paper in front of him and read out your prediction. It says, "Three of clubs." You've successfully predicted the future three times in a row. Expect a lot of invitations to the racetrack.

NOTES

You can dress this trick in lots of different ways. There's no restriction on the kind of things people can think of: names, colors, numbers, places, animals, etc. However, you'll always have to force one of the items, in this case the chosen playing card.

If you don't want to use playing cards, you could use the dice force. You know that if someone throws a pair of dice and adds the top and bottom numbers, they'll always total 14. That's what you write on the first slip of paper. When you get to the third spectator, you ask him to roll the dice and do the addition to arrive at that figure.

I've got another more lighthearted approach to this trick in which no force is used; I employ a bit of humor instead. On the first slip of paper you write the date. By that, I mean that you write down today's date. When you get to the third spectator, ask him to take out a coin from his pocket and hold it tightly in his hand. He should make sure that no one knows what kind of coin he's got. Ask him to hold his closed hand up high as you stare at it. You say, "Now, it would be impossible for me to tell you which coin you've got; it's hidden in your hand and no one can see it." Then you write something on your pad. You're working the one-ahead principle as usual and writing down whatever it was that the second spectator chose. Fold the slip, write the number 2 on its side, and drop it into the cup.

Keep him there holding the coin up in his closed hand. At the finish of the trick, reveal that you got predictions 1 and 2 correct. Everyone should be suitably impressed. Now look at the third spectator. "You were the most difficult. You were the most skeptical. And I wonder if you'd really be impressed if I just told you what coin you're holding in your hand—maybe that's not enough. But what if I could tell you the date? That would be impressive, right?" He'll agree, thinking that you mean the date on the coin. "OK, then. Take a look."

He goes to take a look at the coin, but what you really meant was to take a look at the paper because you now open the third slip and show it to the spectators, saying, "I said I'd tell you the date. And this is it. The Fourth of July!" Sure enough, written across the paper is today's date, whatever it happens to be. That should get a laugh. Finish by complimenting the third spectator: "I know a skeptic when I see one, and I know to quit while I'm ahead—two out of three isn't bad!"

This is a much less serious approach to the routine, but it can be more suitable if you're at a party or bar or in some situation where you just want to have a laugh, rather than selling them the idea that you're in touch with the dark side, or, indeed, when you don't have cards or dice to use for the force.

The routine works really well on special occasions such as Halloween, Easter, Christmas, or New Year's Eve, in which case I modify the last line: "That's the date, December 31, and so I'll take this opportunity to wish you a very happy New Year!" It makes a nice, fun sign-off to the routine.

TRICK 7

Everyone's heard of so-called psychics who claim they can bend spoons using the power of their minds. Well, now you can do it, too. You take an ordinary spoon, stroke it lightly, and the metal mysteriously bends; it's an amazingly convincing illusion to watch. But you can go even further than that. You take another spoon and this time it doesn't just bend; it breaks completely in two!

Some people claim to be able to do this for real. A much easier and more practical way to bend and break spoons is to use sleight-of-hand and psychology. There are two secrets to this illusion because the bending and the breaking of the spoon use completely different methods, so let's look at them one at a time.

The Bend

The only requirement is that the spoon you intend to bend using your mysterious "psychic" powers actually can be bent using just your hands. Most spoons are not very strong and can be bent easily using a little brute force. I suggest you start with teaspoons and work your way up the cutlery chain. It's also much better if a trick like this arises out of some natural conversation. If people know you do tricks, and especially if you've already done some mind reading, they'll almost always want to discuss other strange phenomena.

You won't find it difficult to steer the conversation toward spoon-bending. "Have you seen that guy on TV who bends spoons? Have you ever tried it yourself? No? Let's have a go now, then. Everyone grab a spoon." Involving the whole audience makes this a perfect party trick. When everyone, including you, has a spoon in their hands, the routine begins. "Just hold the spoon in your left hand like this and, with your right fingers, start to stroke it at the neck."

You hold your spoon at the bowl, between the finger and thumb of the left hand (1). Your right hand then comes over the top and strokes it at the neck of the spoon (2). Keep stroking it as if genuinely trying to make it bend and encourage the spectators to do the same. Do this for a few moments until you can see that they're all joining in and genuinely occupied with the futile task in hand.

No matter how hard they try, unless they're cheating, no one's spoon will bend, including yours. What you need is a little bit of misdirection so that you can secretly put a bend in your spoon.

You get it by looking at one of the spectators near you and saying, "No, not like that. Do it like this." You stop stroking your spoon and reach over with your right hand as if to help him. Keep the bowl of the spoon in your left hand. It's more than likely that most people will be holding theirs the opposite way that you are. Give him some phony advice about the right position and then move his hands so that they're closer to what you were demonstrating earlier. Other people

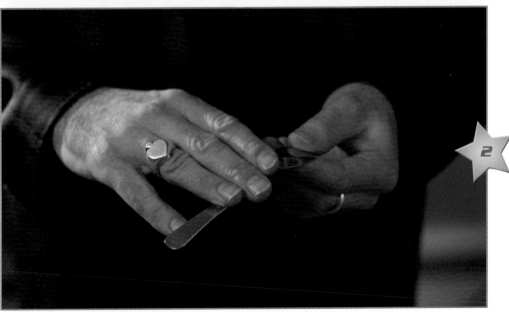

nearby will look at his hands to see how they should be holding their spoons. This is your moment of misdirection—they're not watching you; they're watching someone else or checking that they're following your instructions correctly. Time to make your move. "That's better," you say. Your hands take hold of the spoon once again and, when no one is looking, give it a sharp but subtle bend (3).

You need to do this quickly and without giving away the fact that you're using any pressure on the spoon. Use the minimum movement

possible and bend it at the neck where it's weakest. Don't suddenly yank at the ends of the spoon as if trying to bend the unbendable. Spoons, particularly teaspoons, require an amazingly small amount of strength to bend. You even can hold it in one hand and lever it against the outside of your thigh if it's a thin, weak one.

Immediately the spoon is bent. Now return it to the starting position in your left hand with your fingers and thumb on the inverted bowl. Your right hand hides the bend from view. The spoon is held waist high and the handle is pointing toward the spectators. Continue talking as if nothing has changed. "That's good, keep stroking it and think, 'Bend!' You'll feel it start to get warm." Do this for a few more seconds and then suddenly say, "It's working! Look, I think it's starting to bend." Everyone will stop what they're doing and look at your spoon. Your right hand is still stroking it. When you've got their attention, gradually draw your right fingers off the neck of the spoon, gradually exposing the bend until you're just stroking the neck of the spoon with your middle finger (4, 5, 6). Here's the

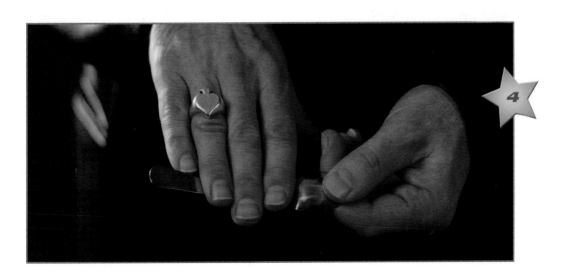

moment where you convince everyone that the spoon actually is bending before their very eyes. Slowly pull back with the left thumb on the bowl of the spoon. The handle of the spoon will start to tip upward (7).

"Look—look at the handle!" Everyone will focus on the handle and, as they do, you tip the bowl upward a little more. The small movement at the bowl of the spoon turns into a larger movement at the handle. The handle slowly rises upward an inch or two and it genuinely looks as if the spoon is bending. It's an amazing optical illusion.

If you slowly turn to your left as you do it, the illusion of the movement of the spoon is really strong. You're almost done. "It's bent. It's definitely bent, isn't it?" Stop stroking the spoon and take it in your right hand by the handle. With your left hand, take a spoon from someone else and hold them both up for everyone to see. The difference is obvious. The only conclusion anyone can come to is that you've just bent a spoon using the power of the mind. Well done!

The Break

The breaking spoon is a great follow-up to the bending spoon, but it requires a bit of preparation. If you know you're going to do this trick, you need to steal a spoon and prepare it in advance. Take it to the bathroom or somewhere private. Hold it between your hands and bend it up and down rapidly (8).

The spoon will get very hot as you do this, so be careful you don't burn yourself—seriously! The bending stresses the metal of the spoon, making it weak. You need to bend it backward and forward enough times to weaken it but not quite break it. If you've got several spoons, it's worth counting the number of bends you make before one snaps, and then repeating it with another spoon but stopping one bend short. It takes some practice to get that judgment right, but if you do, you'll have a spoon that looks completely normal apart from a small hairline fracture at the neck.

Put it somewhere you can find it easily during the routine: under a napkin, on the table, or even in your pocket. Now imagine that you've just performed the bending spoon trick. Everyone's understandably excited. Some people are examining the bent spoon; others are still trying to make their own spoons bend.

You pick up another one—this time it's the one you've prepared earlier—and again you start to show everyone how easy it is to make it bend. Once again you hold the spoon by the bowl and rub it with your right fingers. Everyone's watching you. Rub it for a little while and then say, "Wow, this one's going really fast—quick, hold out your hands." Someone does so and you change the position of the spoon so that you're holding it by the handle in your left hand. Cover the break with your right forefinger and thumb and keep rubbing it there (9).

What you actually do is gradually apply some force with your right thumb and finger, bending the bowl down until it breaks. Sometimes the bowl will just snap off, but sometimes it will dangle for a while as if the neck is melting—this looks great and always gets gasps of amazement (10).

Either way, when it does, you let it fall into the spectator's open hands (11). Pretend to be really excited about this. Your enthusiasm is contagious and it's all part of creating the atmosphere. You want the audience to feel that something really weird has just happened.

NOTES

The most difficult part of the spoon-bending routine is sitting around afterward with your audience and having to answer all their questions about supposed psychic phenomena. Sometimes it can be hard to keep a straight face!

GLOSSARY

graphology Analysis of a person's handwriting.

misdirection This is redirecting the audience's attention to something other than the method of the trick. For example, you might gaze at your left hand during a trick to encourage the audience to believe that a coin is there. Looking in the direction of your left hand discourages the audience from looking at your right hand, where the coin actually is palmed.

mortice key Also known as a skeleton key, it is an antique style of key that is designed to open several different locks.

palming Similar to the classic-palm, palming is holding a coin with the base of the palm.

prophecy A foretelling of the future; a prediction of events in a certain circumstance.

sleight-of-hand Manual dexterity in the performance of magic. People often refer to the quickness of the hands, but speed is rarely of value in magic. More useful is the ability to act naturally while palming or executing some other complex move.

spectators People who are watching a performance; your audience.

upjog If you spread through the deck and raise each ace, for example, as you come to it so that all the aces are sticking up and out of the spread, magicians say that the aces are upjogged. If you were looking for four aces in the deck, you'd spread through the cards, upjog the aces, and then pull them out all at once before placing them on the table.

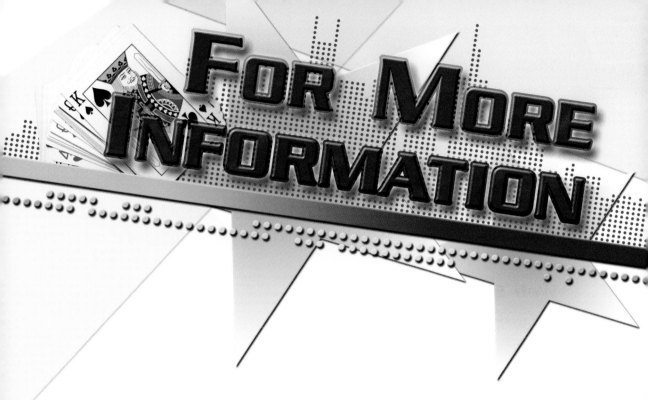

FOR MORE INFORMATION

Magic Max, Inc.
3728 Grissom Lane
Kissimmee, FL 34741
(407) 847-7552
Web site: http://www.magicmax.com

Magic Times
Meir Yedid Magic
P.O. Box 2566
Fair Lawn, NJ 07410
(201) 703-1171
Web site: http://www.magictimes.com

Magic Tricks, Inc.
2768 Columbia Road
Gordonsville, VA 22942
(540) 832-0900
Web site: http://www.magictricks.com

Magic Web Channel
P.O. Box 81391
Las Vegas, NV 89180
(702) 376-4727
Web site: http://www.magicwebchannel.com

Web Sites

Due to the changing nature of Internet links, Rosen Publishing has developed an online list of Web sites related to the subject of this book. This site is updated regularly. Please use this link to access the list:

http://www.rosenlinks.com/am/mmin

FOR FURTHER READING

Copperfield, David. *David Copperfield's Beyond Imagination*. New York, NY: HarperCollins Publishers, 1997.

Kalush, William *The Secret Life of Houdini: The Making of America's First Superhero*. New York, NY: Atria, 2006.

Lemezma, Marc. *Mind Magic: Extraordinary Tricks to Mystify, Baffle and Entertain*. London, England: New Holland, 2005.

Milbourne, Christopher. *The Illustrated History of Magic*. New York, NY: Carroll & Graf, 2005.

Severn, Bill. *Bill Severn's Complete Book of Magic: The Ultimate Book of Fascinating Illusions with Rope, Ribbon, String, Money, Coins & Mental Magic*. New York, NY: Galahad, 1998.

Steinmeyer, Jim. *Art and Artifice: And Other Essays of Illusion*. New York, NY: Carroll & Graf, 2006.

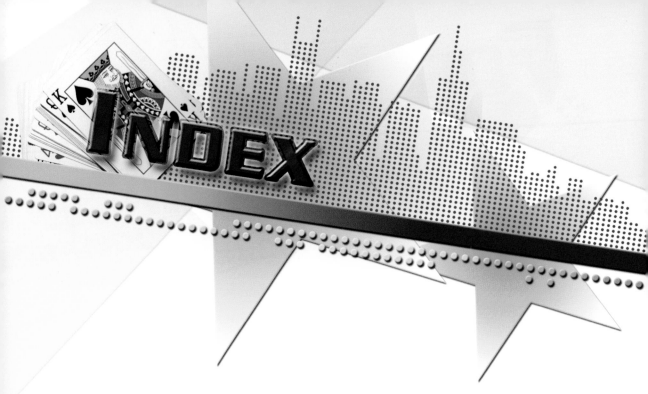

INDEX

About the Author

Paul Zenon has dozens of TV credits to his name, including his own shows *Paul Zenon's Trick or Treat*, *Paul Zenon's Tricky Christmas*, and *White Magic with Paul Zenon*. He also has appeared on many other television shows, including *History of Magic, Secret History—Magic at War, The World's 50 Greatest Magic Tricks*, and many more. Zenon has performed in around thirty countries and in every conceivable location, from the Tropicana Hotel in Las Vegas to the hold of an aircraft carrier in the Adriatic; from the London Palladium to a clearing in the jungles of Belize; from the Magic Castle in Hollywood to the back of a truck in the Bosnian war zone.

Designers: Interior, Nelson Sá; Cover, Tahara Anderson
Editor: Nicholas Croce
Photography: Karl Adamson